What are....?

ISLANDS

Claire Llewellyn

Heinemann
LIBRARY

For more information about Heinemann Library books, or to order, please telephone +44 (0)1865 888066, or send a fax to +44 (0)1865 314091. You can visit our web site at www.heinemann.co.uk

First published in Great Britain by Heinemann Library,
Halley Court, Jordan Hill, Oxford OX2 8EJ
a division of Reed Educational and Professional Publishing Ltd.
Heinemann is a registered trademark of Reed Educational & Professional Publishing Ltd.

OXFORD MELBOURNE AUCKLAND
JOHANNESBURG BLANTYRE GABORONE
IBADAN PORTSMOUTH (NH) USA CHICAGO

Designed by David Oakley
Illustrations by Hardlines (p.8,9) and Jo Brooker
Printed by South China Printing Co.(1988) Ltd, Hong Kong / China

04 03 02 01 00
10 9 8 7 6 5 4 3 2 1

ISBN 0 431 02379 4

British Library Cataloguing in Publication Data

Llewellyn, Claire
  What are islands?
  1. Islands – Juvenile literature
  1. Title II. Islands
  551.4'2

Acknowledgements
The Publishers would like to thank the following for permission to reproduce photographs: Ecoscene: Alan Towse p.19; FLPA: S Jonasson p.11, Ian Cartwright p.12, Silvestris p.13, E&D Hosking p.14; NASA: Johnson Space Centre p.22, p.24, p.26; Oxford Scientific Films: Scott Winer p.4, W Gregory Brown p.5, W Johnson p.10, Stan Osolonski p.16, Frances Furlong/Survival Anglia p.29; Robert Harding Picture Library: Robert Francis p.6; Still Pictures: Yves Thonnerieux p.17, DRA p.20, B&C Alexander p.28; Telegraph Colour Library: Chris Mellor p.7; Trip: W Jacobs p.15, S Grant p.18, C Rennie p.21.

Cover photograph reproduced with permission of Still Pictures.

Every effort has been made to contact copyright holders of any material reproduced in this book. Any omissions will be rectified in subsequent printings if notice is given to the Publisher.

Contents

Some words are shown in bold, **like this**.
You can find out what they mean by looking
in the Glossary.

What is an island?

An island is a piece of land surrounded by water. It may be in a river, a lake or the sea.

This island is surrounded by the sea.

These islands are so small that nobody lives on them.

Some islands are huge, and are home to millions of people. But most islands are very small. They often lie in groups in the sea.

Cut off by water

Some islands, like the British Isles were once joined to larger pieces of land called **continents**. They were cut off when the **sea level** rose.

Ferries carry passengers from Britain to the continent of Europe.

St. Michael's Mount in the UK is cut off from the mainland at high **tide**.

Some pieces of land are islands only at high tide. People can walk to them when the tide is low.

How are islands made?

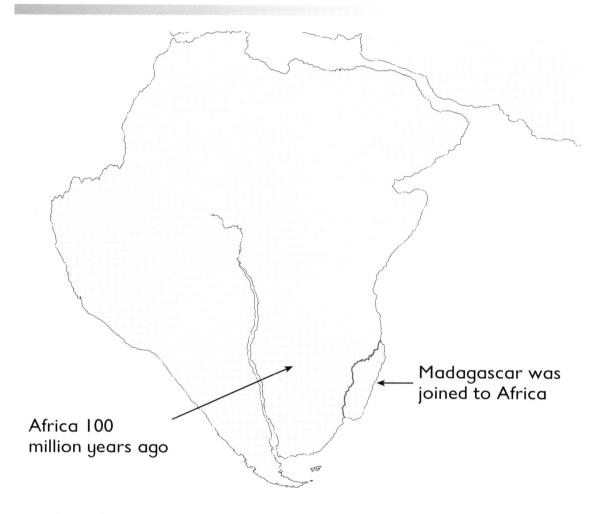

Africa 100
million years ago

Madagascar was
joined to Africa

Madagascar was once part of Africa.

Some islands are made when a piece of land
breaks away from a **continent**. The two pieces
slowly drift apart.

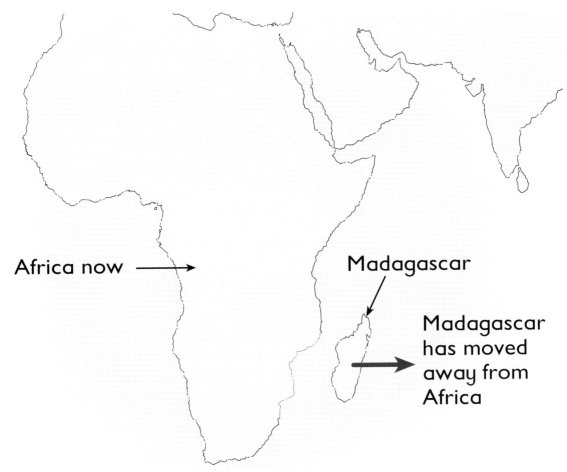

Africa now →

Madagascar

Madagascar has moved away from Africa

When the Earth's surface moved, the land became surrounded by sea.

50 millon years ago, a huge piece of land broke away from the continent of Africa. It became the island of Madagascar.

Volcanoes in the sea

Other islands are the tops of **volcanoes** on the sea-bed. When a volcano **erupts**, hot **lava** pours out and piles up around it. Slowly, the volcano grows bigger.

These islands are the tops of volcanoes under the sea.

After thousands of years, some undersea
volcanoes grow so tall that they reach
the surface. They stick out of the sea.
This makes new islands.

This 'new' island, called Surtsey,
appeared near Iceland in 1963.

Coral islands

Some islands are made of coral. Corals are tiny animals that live in the sea and make rocky **reefs**. Over many thousands of years the reefs pile up to make islands.

Coral reefs are made by billions of tiny animals called corals.

Coral islands are sometimes shaped like a ring. They lie very low in the water, and are often flooded in storms.

You can see how low and flat this island is.

New island life

There are no plants or animals on a new island. As time passes, birds fly to the island. Other animals swim there or float on logs.

Nothing lives or grows on this island.

Birds nest on new islands, and seeds take root on the shore.

Seeds are blown to the new island on the wind or are washed up by the sea. They start to grow in the sand.

Island animals

Galapagos penguins are not used to people. They have no fear of them.

Many islands are far from the nearest land. The animals on the islands have never been hunted by other animals or by people. This has helped them to survive.

Some island animals live nowhere else in the world. This makes them very rare.

The giant tortoise is only found on the Galapagos Islands.

Away from it all

Many islands are quiet places. They are far from cities, motorways and modern life. This makes them good places for wildlife.

This island in Florida is a safe place for pelicans to raise their young.

These islands near Australia have many visitors.

Many people enjoy taking their holidays on islands. Visitors need hotels and restaurants. This brings jobs to the islands but people also need to protect the islands and their wildlife.

Living on islands

Some countries are made up of islands. Japan is made up of 3900 islands, but most people live on the four biggest islands.

Thousands of islands make up the country of Japan.

People travel between Japan's islands on this 'bullet train'.

Long bridges and tunnels have been built between the islands of Japan. People and goods can reach every part of the country.

Island map 1

This is a photo of an island. It was taken from a **satellite**. The island is surrounded by the sea.

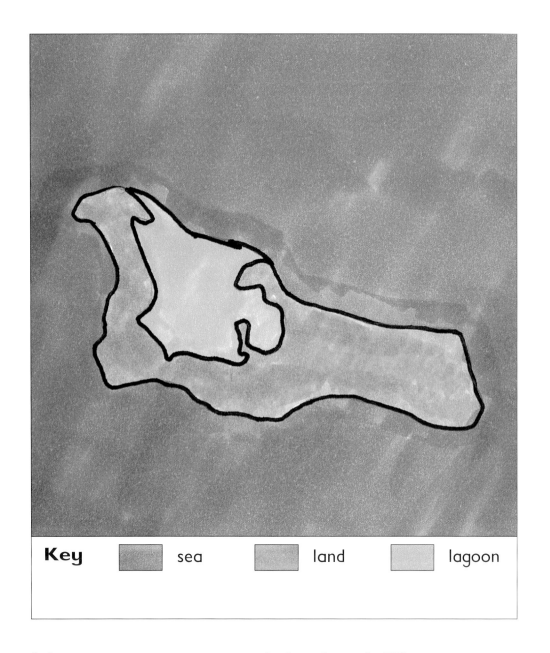

Key ▮ sea ▮ land ▮ lagoon

Maps are pictures of the land. This map shows us the same place as the photo. The key tells us what each colour means.

Island map 2

The island looks bigger in this photo. You can see that there are buildings on some parts of the island. There are beaches and coral **reefs** around the shore.

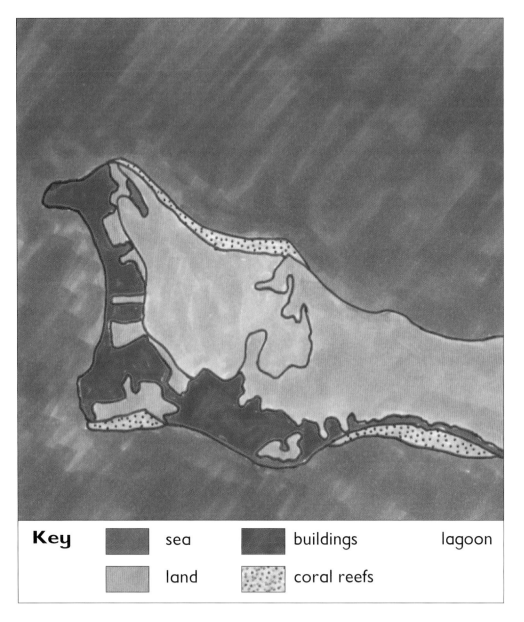

Key

■	sea	■	buildings	lagoon
■	land	::::	coral reefs	

The buildings are shown in red. You can see that there are very few buildings in the middle of the island. Most of them are along the shore.

Island map 3

This photo is even closer. You can see about half the island. You can see buildings and roads. At the top of the island is a large **lagoon**. A lagoon is a sheltered area of water surrounded by a coral **reef**.

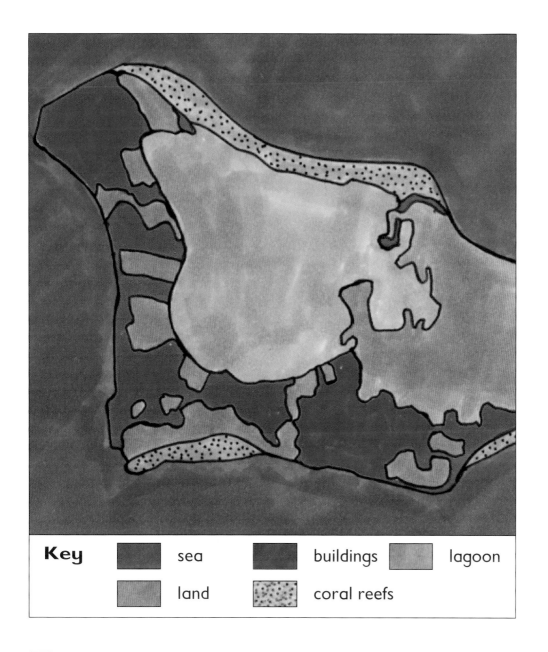

Key

■	sea	■	buildings	▦	lagoon
▦	land	▦	coral reefs		

Tha lagoon is shown in blue. It is a lighter blue than the sea because the water is shallower here.

Amazing island facts

Greenland is the world's largest island. It is six times bigger than Germany and four times bigger than Spain. Most of Greenland is covered with thick sheets of ice.

Tristan da Cunha is the world's most faraway island. It is home to about 200 people. They live 2740 kilometres from the nearest **continent** – that's a five-hour journey by plane.

Glossary

continent a very large piece of land. There are seven continents on Earth.

erupt to suddenly shoot out lava and ash from deep inside the Earth

lagoon the sheltered shallow water that lies behind a coral reef

lava the hot rock that shoots out of a volcano

reef tiny animals called corals live in the sea. Their skeletons build up to make reefs.

satellite a special machine that goes around the Earth in space. It can take photographs of the Earth.

sea level the usual level of the sea

tide the sea level goes up and down each day

volcano a mountain made out of lava. It sometimes erupts and shoots out hot rock and ash from inside the Earth.

More books to read

Nicola Baxter. *Our Wonderful Earth.*
Two-Can, 1997

Andy Owen and Miranda Ashwell.
What Are...Seas and Oceans?
Heinemann, 1998

Rosanne Hooper and Monica Byles. *Islands.*
Two-Can, 1992

You may need help to read this book on islands:

Terry Jennings. *Our Earth: Coasts and Islands.*
Belitha Press, 1989

Index